MARKS &
SPENCER

soups

simple and delicious easy-to-make recipes

Marks and Spencer p.l.c.
PO Box 3339,
Chester, CH99 9QS

www.marksandspencer.com

ISBN: 1-84461-489-1

Printed in China

This edition designed by Talking Design, Worthing

NOTES FOR THE READER

- This book uses both metric and imperial measurements. Follow the same units of
  measurement throughout; do not mix metric and imperial.
- All spoon measurements are level: teaspoons are assumed to be 5 ml, and tablespoons
  are assumed to be 15 ml.
- Unless otherwise stated, milk is assumed to be full fat, eggs and individual vegetables
  such as potatoes are medium, and pepper is freshly ground black pepper.
- Recipes using raw or very lightly cooked eggs should be avoided by infants, the elderly,
  pregnant women, convalescents, and anyone suffering from an illness.
- Optional ingredients, variations or serving suggestions have not been included in the
  calculations.
- The times given are an approximate guide only. Preparation times differ according to the
  techniques used by different people and the cooking times vary as a result of the type of
  oven used.

contents

introduction

There is no substitute for good, home-made soup, and creating soups at home can be tremendously enjoyable. You need little in the way of basic equipment, just a large saucepan with a lid and a sharp knife for chopping. A large frying pan or wok is also helpful, but not essential.

Soup can be very economical to make – you can use leftovers to make some delicious concoctions, from light starters and snacks to more substantial soups that are meals in themselves. On special occasions, you can splash out on more expensive ingredients and create impressive soups that will grace any dinner table.

Soups are very nutritious, too, and can be packed with healthy ingredients such as vegetables, fish, pulses and rice. Many are low in fat, and high-fat ingredients such as cream can be replaced with lower fat alternatives.

Soup is also a popular international food. Many of the recipes included in this book reflect the rich diversity of the different cuisines found across the world, so wherever you happen to be – and whatever the occasion – you are bound to find something in its pages to satisfy your taste and delight your dinner guests.

guide to recipe key

 CATEGORY
Recipes are graded as follows:
1 pea = easy, 2 peas = very easy, 3 peas = extremely easy.

 SERVES 4
Recipes generally serve four people. Simply halve the ingredients to serve two, taking care not to mix imperial and metric measurements.

 10 MINUTES
Preparation time.

 10 MINUTES
Cooking time.

vegetable soups

Vegetables are very healthy foods and make nutritious, satisfying ingredients in soups. The combinations of texture and flavour in this section are endless. From the chilled Gazpacho, with its ripe tomatoes and red peppers, to the delightful Vegetable Soup with Pesto, packed with fresh basil and garlic, there are mouthwatering recipes for every season using every type of vegetable. Alcohol is also a great favourite in soups, so why not try the Mushroom & Sherry Soup? And for cheese lovers, the Sweet Potato & Stilton Soup is an absolute must.

fresh tomato soup

1 tbsp olive oil
650 g/1 lb 7 oz plum
 tomatoes
1 onion, cut into quarters
1 garlic clove, sliced thinly
1 celery stick, chopped
 coarsely

500 ml/18 fl oz vegetable
 or chicken stock
55 g/2 oz dried anellini
 or other soup pasta
salt and pepper
fresh flat-leaf parsley,
 chopped, to garnish

Pour the olive oil into a large, heavy-based saucepan and add the tomatoes, onion, garlic and celery. Cover and cook over a low heat for 45 minutes, occasionally shaking the saucepan gently, until the mixture is pulpy.

Transfer the mixture to a food processor or blender and process to a smooth purée. Push the purée through a sieve into a clean saucepan.

Add the stock and bring to the boil. Add the pasta, bring back to the boil and cook for 8-10 minutes, until the pasta is tender, but still firm to the bite. Season to taste with salt and pepper. Ladle into warmed bowls, sprinkle with the parsley and serve immediately.

onion soup with croûtons

100 g/3½ oz butter
2 garlic cloves, crushed
3 large onions,
  thinly sliced
1 tsp sugar
2 tbsp plain flour
225 ml/8 fl oz dry
  white wine

1.5 litres/2¾ pints
  vegetable stock
salt and pepper
CROÛTONS
2 tbsp olive oil
2 slices day-old white
  bread, crusts removed
thick slices of fresh

wholemeal and white
bread, to serve

Melt the butter in a large saucepan over a medium heat. Add the garlic, onions and sugar and cook, stirring, for about 25 minutes, until the onions have caramelised.

In a bowl, mix the flour with enough wine to make a smooth paste, then stir it into the onion mixture. Cook for 2 minutes, then stir in the remaining wine and the stock. Season with salt and pepper. Bring to the boil, then reduce the heat, cover the pan and simmer for 30 minutes.

Meanwhile, to make the croûtons, heat the oil in a frying pan until hot. Cut the bread into small cubes and cook over a high heat, stirring, for about 2 minutes, until crisp and golden. Remove from the heat, drain the croûtons on kitchen paper and reserve.

When the soup is cooked, remove from the heat and ladle into serving bowls. Scatter over some fried croûtons and serve with slices of wholemeal and white bread.

VERY EASY   **SERVES 4 - 6**   **10 MINUTES**   **25 - 30 MINUTES**

leek & potato soup

55 g/2 oz butter
1 onion, chopped
3 leeks, sliced
225 g/8 oz potatoes,
  peeled and cut into
  2-cm/¾-inch cubes
850 ml/1½ pints
  vegetable stock

salt and pepper
150 ml/5 fl oz
  single cream, optional
2 tbsp snipped fresh
  chives, to garnish

Melt the butter in a large saucepan over a medium heat, add the prepared vegetables and sauté gently for 2–3 minutes until soft but not brown. Pour in the stock, bring to the boil, then reduce the heat and simmer, covered, for 15 minutes.

Remove from the heat and liquidise the soup in the saucepan using a hand-held stick blender if you have one. Otherwise, pour into a blender, liquidise until smooth and return to the rinsed-out saucepan.

Heat the soup, season with salt and pepper to taste and serve in warm bowls, swirled with the cream, if using, and garnished with chives.

vegetable soup with pesto

2 tbsp olive oil
2 garlic cloves, chopped
2 onions, chopped
1 celery stick, trimmed
 and chopped
1 carrot, peeled and chopped
1.2 litres/2 pints
 vegetable stock
1 potato, peeled and chopped

175 g/6 oz frozen peas
400 g/14 oz canned
 cannellini beans, drained
salt and pepper
1 tbsp chopped fresh basil
sprigs of fresh basil,
 to garnish
fresh focaccia, to serve

PESTO
2 garlic cloves, chopped
25 g/1 oz fresh basil leaves
85 g/3 oz Parmesan
 cheese, grated
5 tbsp extra-virgin olive oil
100 g/3½ oz pine kernels

Heat 2 tablespoons of olive oil in a large saucepan over a low heat.
Add the garlic and onions and cook, stirring, for 3 minutes, until
slightly softened. Add the celery and carrot and cook for a further
5 minutes, stirring. Pour in the stock, then add the potato, peas and
beans. Season with salt and pepper. Bring to the boil, then reduce the
heat, cover the pan and simmer for 30 minutes.

Meanwhile, to make the pesto, put all the ingredients into a food processor
and blend until smooth.

Stir the chopped basil into the soup and cook for a further 5 minutes.
Remove from the heat and ladle into serving bowls. Garnish each bowl
with a generous tablespoonful of pesto and a sprig of basil and serve
with fresh focaccia.

mushroom & sherry soup

4 tbsp butter
2 garlic cloves, chopped
3 onions, sliced
450 g/1 lb mixed white and
 chestnut mushrooms, sliced
100 g/3½ oz fresh ceps or
 porcini mushrooms, sliced

3 tbsp chopped
 fresh parsley
500 ml/18 fl oz
 vegetable stock
salt and pepper
3 tbsp plain flour
125 ml/4 fl oz milk
2 tbsp sherry

125 ml/4 fl oz soured cream
soured cream and chopped
 fresh parsley, to garnish
fresh crusty rolls, to serve

Melt the butter in a large saucepan over a low heat. Add the garlic and onions and cook, stirring, for 3 minutes, until slightly softened. Add the mushrooms and cook for a further 5 minutes, stirring. Add the chopped parsley, pour in the stock and season with salt and pepper. Bring to the boil, then reduce the heat, cover the pan and simmer for 20 minutes.

Put the flour into a bowl, mix in enough milk to make a smooth paste, then stir it into the soup. Cook, stirring, for 5 minutes. Stir in the remaining milk and the sherry and cook for a further 5 minutes. Remove from the heat and stir in the soured cream. Return the pan to the heat and warm gently.

Remove from the heat and ladle into serving bowls. Garnish with soured cream and chopped fresh parsley, and serve with fresh crusty rolls.

VERY EASY   **SERVES 4**    **15 - 20 MINUTES + 10 MINUTES COOLING**   **55 MINUTES - 1 HOUR**

creamy carrot & parsnip soup

4 tbsp butter
1 large onion, chopped
450 g/1 lb carrots,
  peeled and chopped
2 large parsnips, peeled
  and chopped
1 tbsp grated fresh
  root ginger

1 tsp grated orange rind
600 ml/1 pint
  vegetable stock
125 ml/4 fl oz
  single cream
black pepper and
  coriander, to garnish

sprigs of fresh coriander
fresh crusty rolls, to serve

Melt the butter in a large saucepan over a low heat. Add the onion and cook, stirring, for 3 minutes, until slightly softened. Add the carrots and parsnips, cover the pan and cook, stirring occasionally, for about 15 minutes, until the vegetables have softened a little. Stir in the ginger, orange rind and stock. Bring to the boil, then reduce the heat, cover the pan and simmer for 30–35 minutes until the vegetables are tender. Remove from the heat and leave to cool for 10 minutes.

Transfer the soup into a food processor and blend until smooth (you may need to do this in batches). Return the soup to the saucepan, stir in the cream and season well with salt and pepper. Warm through gently over a low heat.

Remove from the heat and ladle into soup bowls. Garnish each bowl with black pepper and a sprig of coriander and serve the soup with fresh crusty rolls.

sweet potato & stilton soup

4 tbsp butter
1 large onion, chopped
2 leeks, trimmed
  and sliced
175 g/6 oz sweet
  potatoes, peeled
  and diced

850 ml/1½ pints
  vegetable stock
1 tbsp chopped
  fresh parsley
1 bay leaf
pepper
150 ml/5 fl oz
  double cream

150 g/5½ oz Stilton
  cheese, crumbled
2 tbsp finely crumbled
  Stilton cheese and
  chopped parsley,
  to garnish
slices of fresh bread,
  to serve

Melt the butter in a large saucepan over a medium heat. Add the onion
and leeks and cook, stirring, for about 3 minutes, until slightly softened.
Add the sweet potatoes and cook for a further 5 minutes, stirring, then
pour in the stock, add the parsley and bay leaf and season with pepper.
Bring to the boil, then lower the heat, cover the pan and simmer for about
30 minutes. Remove from the heat and leave to cool for 10 minutes.
Remove the bay leaf.

Transfer half of the soup into a food processor and blend until smooth.
Return to the pan with the rest of the soup, stir in the cream and cook
for a further 5 minutes. Gradually stir in the crumbled Stilton until
melted (do not let the soup boil).

Remove from the heat and ladle into serving bowls. Garnish with finely
crumbled Stilton and serve with slices of fresh bread.

 **EXTREMELY EASY**  **SERVES 4** **15 MINUTES +
2 - 3 HOURS
CHILLING** **0 MINUTES**

gazpacho

500 g/1 lb 2 oz large
  ripe tomatoes
4 tbsp extra-virgin olive oil
3 spring onions, trimmed
  and chopped
2 red peppers, deseeded
  and chopped

3 garlic cloves, chopped
1 cucumber, peeled
  and chopped
1 tbsp red wine vinegar
1 tbsp chopped
  mixed herbs
salt and pepper

croûtons and sprigs of
  fresh basil and olive oil,
  to garnish

First, skin the tomatoes. Bring a kettle of water to the boil, put the tomatoes into a heatproof bowl, then pour over enough boiling water to cover them. Let them soak for about 3 minutes, then lift them out of the water and leave to cool slightly. When the tomatoes are cool enough to handle, gently pierce the skins with the point of a knife. Remove and discard the skins.

Halve the tomatoes and remove the seeds. Chop the flesh and put it into a food processor. Add the oil, spring onions, red peppers, garlic, cucumber, vinegar and mixed herbs to the food processor. Season with salt and pepper and blend until smooth. Strain the blended mixture through a sieve into a large bowl, then cover with clingfilm and refrigerate for 2–3 hours.

Ladle the chilled soup into serving bowls and garnish with croûtons and sprigs of fresh basil.

seafood soups

Fish and shellfish are very nutritious and quick to cook. Many are low in calories and fat, yet rich in protein and nutrients such as B vitamins. They are also an excellent source of iodine, which helps to maintain a healthy thyroid gland and keeps the metabolism running efficiently. Above all, however, fish and shellfish are delicious, and impart a wonderful richness to soups. Always buy the freshest you can find, and you will be rewarded with soups that are unparalleled in terms of quality and flavour.

traditional salmon soup

2 tbsp butter
1 onion, chopped
1 leek, trimmed
  and sliced
1 tbsp plain flour
700 ml/¼ pints fish stock
1 large potato, peeled
  and chopped

1 tbsp chopped fresh
  parsley
1 tbsp chopped fresh dill
salt and pepper
300 g/10½ oz skinless
  salmon fillets, cut into
  bite-sized pieces
2 egg yolks

100 ml/3½ fl oz
  double cream
sprigs of fresh dill,
  to garnish

Melt the butter in a large pan over a medium heat. Add the onion and leek and cook, stirring, for 3 minutes, until slightly softened. In a bowl, mix the flour with enough stock to make a smooth paste and stir it into the pan. Cook, stirring, for 1 minute, then gradually stir in the remaining stock with the potato, parsley and dill. Season with salt and pepper. Bring to the boil, then lower the heat, cover the pan and simmer for 25 minutes.

Add the salmon to the pan and cook for about 6 minutes until cooked through. In a clean bowl, whisk together the egg yolks and cream, then stir into the soup.

Remove from the heat and ladle into serving bowls. Garnish with sprigs of fresh dill.

haddock & prawn chowder

1 tbsp butter
1 onion, chopped
3 tbsp plain flour
500 ml/18 fl oz fish stock
1 bay leaf
salt and pepper
500 ml/18 fl oz milk
2 tbsp dry white wine

juice and grated rind of
  1 lemon
450 g/1 lb haddock
  fillets, skinned
125 g/4½ oz frozen
  sweetcorn, defrosted
250 g/9 oz prawns,
  cooked and peeled

200 ml/7 fl oz
  double cream
whole cooked prawns,
  to garnish
fresh wholemeal bread
  and fresh green salad,
  to serve

Melt the butter in a large saucepan over a medium heat. Add the onion and cook, stirring, for about 3 minutes, until slightly softened. In a bowl, mix the flour with enough stock to make a smooth paste and stir it into the pan. Cook, stirring, for 2 minutes, then gradually stir in the remaining stock. Add the bay leaf and season with salt and pepper. Bring to the boil, then lower the heat. Pour in the milk and wine, and stir in the lemon juice and grated rind. Simmer for 15 minutes.

Rinse the haddock under cold running water, then drain and cut into bite-sized chunks. Add them to the soup with the sweetcorn. Cook for 15 minutes, until the fish is tender and cooked through. Stir in the prawns and the cream. Cook for a further 2–3 minutes, then remove from the heat and discard the bay leaf.

Ladle into serving bowls, garnish with whole cooked prawns and serve with fresh wholemeal bread and a fresh green salad.

sweetcorn & crab soup

2 tbsp vegetable or
   groundnut oil
4 garlic cloves,
   chopped finely
5 shallots, chopped finely
2 lemongrass stalks,
   chopped finely
2.5-cm/1-inch piece fresh
   root ginger, chopped finely

1 litre/1¾ pints
   chicken stock
400 g/14 oz canned
   coconut milk
225 g/8 oz frozen
   sweetcorn kernels
350 g/12 oz canned
   crab meat, drained
   and shredded

2 tbsp fish sauce
juice of 1 lime
1 tsp palm sugar or soft,
   light brown sugar
bunch of fresh coriander,
   chopped, to garnish

Heat the oil in a large frying pan and fry the garlic, shallots, lemongrass
and ginger over a low heat, stirring occasionally, for 2–3 minutes, until
softened. Add the stock and coconut milk and bring to the boil. Add the
sweetcorn, lower the heat and simmer gently for 3–4 minutes.

Add the crab meat, fish sauce, lime juice and sugar and simmer gently
for 1 minute. Ladle into warmed bowls, garnish with the chopped
coriander and serve immediately.

EASY SERVES 4  20 MINUTES +
10 MINUTES
SOAKING 45 MINUTES

bouillabaisse

100 ml/3½ fl oz olive oil
3 garlic cloves, chopped
2 onions, chopped
2 tomatoes, deseeded
  and chopped
700 ml/1¼ pints
  fish stock
400 ml/14 fl oz white wine

1 bay leaf
pinch of saffron threads
2 tbsp chopped fresh basil
2 tbsp chopped fresh parsley
200 g/7 oz live mussels
250 g/9 oz snapper or
  monkfish fillets

250 g/9 oz haddock
  fillets, skinned
200 g/7 oz prawns,
  peeled and deveined
100 g/3½ oz scallops
salt and pepper
fresh baguettes, to serve

Heat the oil in a large pan over a medium heat. Add the garlic and onions
and cook, stirring, for 3 minutes. Stir in the tomatoes, stock, wine, bay
leaf, saffron and herbs. Bring to the boil, reduce the heat, cover and
simmer for 30 minutes. Meanwhile, soak the mussels in lightly salted
water for 10 minutes. Scrub the shells under cold running water and pull
off any beards. Discard any with broken shells. Tap the remaining mussels
and discard any that refuse to close. Put the rest into a large pan with a
little water, bring to the boil and cook over a high heat for 4 minutes.
Remove from the heat and discard any that remain closed.

When the tomato mixture is cooked, rinse the fish, pat dry and cut into
chunks. Add to the pan and simmer for 5 minutes. Add the mussels, prawns
and scallops and season. Cook for 3 minutes, until the fish is cooked through.
Remove from the heat, discard the bay leaf and ladle into serving bowls.
Serve with fresh baguettes.

genoese fish soup

25 g/1 oz butter
1 onion, chopped
1 garlic clove,
 finely chopped
55 g/2 oz rindless
 streaky bacon, diced
2 celery sticks, chopped

400 g/14 oz canned
 chopped tomatoes
150 ml/5 fl oz dry white wine
300 ml/10 fl oz fish stock
4 fresh basil leaves, torn
2 tbsp chopped fresh
 flat-leaf parsley
salt and pepper

450 g/1 lb white fish fillets,
 such as cod or monkfish,
 skinned and chopped
115 g/4 oz cooked peeled
 prawns

Melt the butter in a large, heavy-based saucepan. Add the chopped onion
and garlic and cook over a low heat, stirring occasionally, for 5 minutes,
or until softened.

Add the streaky bacon and celery and cook, stirring frequently, for a
further 2 minutes.

Add the tomatoes and their juices, the wine, stock, basil and 1 tablespoon
of the parsley. Season to taste with salt and pepper. Bring to the boil, then
reduce the heat and simmer for 10 minutes.

Add the fish and cook for 5 minutes, or until it is opaque. Add the
prawns and heat through gently for 3 minutes. Ladle into a warmed tureen,
garnish with the remaining chopped parsley and serve immediately.

quick clam chowder

2 tsp sunflower oil
115 g/4 oz rindless
  streaky bacon, diced
25 g/1 oz butter
1 onion, chopped
2 celery sticks, chopped
2 potatoes, chopped

salt and pepper
2 leeks, sliced
400 g/14 oz canned
  chopped tomatoes
3 tbsp chopped fresh
  parsley
1.2 litres/2 pints
  fish stock

550 g/1 lb 4 oz canned
  clams, drained and rinsed

Heat the oil in a heavy-based saucepan. Add the bacon and cook over a medium heat, stirring, for 5 minutes, or until the fat runs and it begins to crisp. Remove from the saucepan, drain on kitchen paper and reserve.

Add the butter to the saucepan and stir to melt. Add the onion, celery and potatoes with a pinch of salt. Cover and cook over a low heat, stirring occasionally, for 10 minutes, or until soft.

Stir in the leeks, the tomatoes and their juices and 2 tablespoons of the parsley. Pour in the stock, bring to the boil, reduce the heat and simmer for 10–15 minutes, or until the vegetables are tender. Season to taste with salt and pepper and stir in the clams. Heat the soup through gently for 2–3 minutes, then ladle into warmed bowls, garnish with the remaining parsley and reserved bacon and serve.

prawn & vegetable bisque

3 tbsp butter
1 garlic clove, chopped
1 onion, sliced
1 carrot, peeled and
chopped
1 celery stick, trimmed
and sliced

1.2 litres/2 pints
fish stock
4 tbsp red wine
1 tbsp tomato purée
1 bay leaf
salt and pepper
600 g/1 lb 5 oz prawns,
peeled and deveined

100 ml/3½ fl oz
double cream
swirls of single cream
and chives, to garnish

Melt the butter in a large saucepan over a medium heat. Add the garlic and onion and cook, stirring, for 3 minutes, until slightly softened. Add the carrot and celery and cook for a further 3 minutes, stirring. Pour in the stock and red wine, then add the tomato purée and bay leaf. Season with salt and pepper. Bring to the boil, then lower the heat and simmer for 20 minutes. Remove from the heat and leave to cool for 10 minutes, then remove and discard the bay leaf.

Transfer half of the soup into a food processor and blend until smooth (you may need to do this in batches). Return to the pan with the rest of the soup. Add the prawns and cook over a low heat for 5–6 minutes.

Stir in the cream and cook for a further 2 minutes, then remove from the heat and ladle into serving bowls. Garnish with single cream and chives and serve at once.

EASY   **SERVES 4**   **10 MINUTES**   **1 HOUR 15 MINUTES – 1 HOUR 30 MINUTES**

chorizo & scallop soup

125 g/4½ oz lean
chorizo, skinned
and chopped
450 g/1 lb split
yellow peas
1 tbsp vegetable oil
2 shallots, chopped
2 carrots, chopped

2 leeks, trimmed
and chopped
2 garlic cloves, chopped
1.5 litres/2¾ pints
vegetable stock
½ tsp dried oregano
salt and pepper
225 g/8 oz scallops

fresh flat-leaf parsley,
chopped, to garnish
slices of fresh wholemeal
bread, to serve

Put the chorizo in a clean, dry frying pan and cook over a medium heat
for about 5–8 minutes. Lift out with a slotted spoon and drain on kitchen
paper. Put the peas in a colander and rinse under cold running water.
Leave to drain.

Heat the oil in a large saucepan over a medium heat. Add the shallots
and cook for about 4 minutes, until slightly softened. Add the carrots,
leeks and garlic and cook for another 3 minutes.

Add the drained peas to the pan, then the stock and oregano. Bring to
the boil, then add the chorizo and season with salt and pepper. Lower
the heat, cover and simmer for 1–1¼ hours. Just before the end of the
cooking time, add the scallops and cook for about 2 minutes.

Remove the saucepan from the heat. Ladle the soup into serving bowls,
garnish with chopped fresh parsley and serve with slices of fresh
wholemeal bread.

mixed fish soup

1 tbsp butter	2 tbsp dry sherry	150 g/5½ oz canned
2 shallots, chopped	2 tbsp lemon juice	sweetcorn, drained
1 leek, trimmed and sliced	300 g/10½ oz haddock	200 ml/7 fl oz
3 tbsp plain flour	fillets, skinned	double cream
500 ml/18 fl oz fish stock	300 g/10½ oz cod fillets,	sprigs of fresh dill and
1 bay leaf	skinned	wedges of lemon,
salt and pepper	200 g/7 oz canned or	to garnish
500 ml/18 fl oz milk	freshly cooked crabmeat	fresh crusty rolls, to serve

Melt the butter in a large saucepan over a medium heat. Add the shallots and leek and cook, stirring, for about 3 minutes, until slightly softened. In a bowl, mix the flour with enough stock to make a smooth paste, then stir it into the pan. Cook, stirring, for 2 minutes, then gradually stir in the remaining stock. Add the bay leaf and season with salt and pepper. Bring to the boil, then lower the heat. Pour in the milk and sherry, and stir in the lemon juice. Simmer for 15 minutes.

Rinse the haddock and cod fillets under cold running water, then drain and cut into bite-sized chunks. Add to the soup with the crabmeat and sweetcorn. Cook for 15 minutes, until the fish is tender and cooked through. Stir in the cream. Cook for another 2–3 minutes, then remove from the heat and discard the bay leaf.

Ladle into serving bowls, garnish with sprigs of fresh dill and lemon wedges and serve with fresh crusty rolls.

poultry &
meat soups

The recipes in this section draw from a wide variety of ingredients and dishes from around the world, such as Scotch Broth and Middle Eastern Soup with Harissa. There is also a continental-style Beef and Bean Soup, and a Pork & Vegetable Broth bursting with delicious Thai flavours. And for the cost-conscious among you, the Turkey & Lentil Soup provides an excellent way of using leftover turkey at Christmas or at other times during the year. You can also substitute leftover chicken for the turkey whenever the need arises.

VERY EASY **SERVES 4** **15 MINUTES +**
10 MINUTES
COOLING **40 MINUTES**

cream of chicken soup

3 tbsp butter
4 shallots, chopped
1 leek, trimmed
and sliced
450 g/1 lb skinless
chicken breasts,
chopped

600 ml/1 pint
chicken stock
1 tbsp chopped
fresh parsley
1 tbsp chopped
fresh thyme
salt and pepper

175 ml/6 fl oz
double cream
sprigs of fresh thyme,
to garnish
fresh crusty rolls,
to serve

Melt the butter in a large saucepan over a medium heat. Add the
shallots and cook, stirring, for 3 minutes, until slightly softened. Add
the leek and cook for a further 5 minutes, stirring. Add the chicken, stock
and herbs, and season with salt and pepper. Bring to the boil, then lower
the heat and simmer for 25 minutes, until the chicken is tender and cooked
through. Remove from the heat and leave to cool for 10 minutes.

Transfer the soup into a food processor and blend until smooth (you may
need to do this in batches). Return the soup to the pan and warm over a
low heat for 5 minutes.

Stir in the cream and cook for a further 2 minutes, then remove from
the heat and ladle into serving bowls. Garnish with sprigs of thyme and
serve with fresh crusty rolls.

VERY EASY   **SERVES 4**   **20 MINUTES**   **50 MINUTES**

turkey & lentil soup

1 tbsp olive oil
1 garlic clove, chopped
1 large onion, chopped
200 g/7 oz mushrooms,
  sliced
1 red pepper, deseeded
  and chopped
6 tomatoes, skinned,
  deseeded and chopped

1.2 litre/2 pints
  chicken stock
150 ml/5 fl oz red wine
85 g/3 oz cauliflower
  florets
1 carrot, peeled and
  chopped
200 g/7 oz red lentils
salt and pepper

350 g/12 oz cooked
  turkey meat, chopped
1 courgette, trimmed
  and chopped
1 tbsp shredded
  fresh basil
basil leaves, to garnish
thick slices of fresh
  crusty bread, to serve

Heat the oil in a large saucepan. Add the garlic and onion and cook over a medium heat, stirring, for 3 minutes, until slightly softened. Add the mushrooms, red pepper and tomatoes and cook for a further 5 minutes, stirring. Pour in the stock and red wine, then add the cauliflower, carrot and red lentils. Season with salt and pepper. Bring to the boil, then lower the heat and simmer the soup gently for 25 minutes, until the vegetables are tender and cooked through.

Add the turkey and courgette to the pan and cook for 10 minutes. Stir in the shredded basil and cook for a further 5 minutes, then remove from the heat and ladle into serving bowls. Garnish with basil leaves and serve with fresh crusty bread.

chicken & potato soup with bacon

1 tbsp butter
2 garlic cloves, chopped
1 onion, sliced
250 g/9 oz smoked lean
 back bacon, chopped
2 large leeks, trimmed
 and sliced
2 tbsp plain flour

1 litre/1¾ pints
 chicken stock
800 g/1 lb 12 oz
 potatoes, peeled
 and chopped
200 g/7 oz skinless
 chicken breast, chopped
salt and pepper

4 tbsp double cream
grilled bacon and flat-leaf
 parsley, to garnish
fresh crusty rolls,
 to serve

Melt the butter in a large saucepan over a medium heat. Add the garlic and onion and cook, stirring, for 3 minutes, until slightly softened. Add the chopped bacon and leeks and cook for a further 3 minutes, stirring. In a bowl, mix the flour with enough stock to make a smooth paste, then stir it into the pan. Cook, stirring, for 2 minutes. Pour in the remaining stock, then add the potatoes and chicken. Season with salt and pepper. Bring to the boil, then lower the heat and simmer for 25 minutes, until the chicken and potatoes are tender and cooked through.

Stir in the cream and cook for a further 2 minutes, then remove from the heat and ladle into serving bowls. Garnish with flat-leaf parsley and serve with crusty rolls.

VERY EASY   **SERVES 4**   **15 MINUTES**   **50 MINUTES**

sausage & red cabbage soup

2 tbsp olive oil
1 garlic clove, chopped
1 large onion, chopped
1 large leek, trimmed
 and sliced
2 tbsp cornflour
1 litre/1¾ pints
 vegetable stock

450 g/1 lb potatoes,
 peeled and sliced
200 g/7 oz skinless
 sausages, sliced
salt and pepper
150 g/5½ oz red
 cabbage, chopped

200 g/7 oz canned black-eyed
 beans, drained
125 ml/4 fl oz double cream
ground paprika, to garnish
fresh crusty rolls, to serve

Heat the oil in a large saucepan. Add the garlic and onion and cook over
a medium heat, stirring, for 3 minutes, until slightly softened. Add the leek
and cook for a further 3 minutes, stirring. In a bowl, mix the cornflour with
enough stock to make a smooth paste, then stir it into the pan. Cook, stirring,
for 2 minutes. Stir in the remaining stock, then add the potatoes and sausages.
Season with salt and pepper. Bring to the boil, then lower the heat and simmer
for 25 minutes.

Add the red cabbage and beans and cook for 10 minutes, then stir in the
cream and cook for a further 5 minutes. Remove from the heat and ladle into
serving bowls. Garnish with ground paprika and serve with fresh crusty rolls.

scotch broth

700 g/1 lb 9 oz neck of lamb
1.7 litres/3 pints water
55 g/2 oz pearl barley
2 onions, chopped
1 garlic clove,
  finely chopped
3 small turnips, cut into
  small dice

3 carrots, peeled and
  finely sliced
2 celery sticks, sliced
2 leeks, sliced
salt and pepper
2 tbsp chopped fresh
  parsley, to garnish

Cut the meat into small pieces, removing as much fat as possible.
Put into a large saucepan and cover with the water. Bring to the boil
over a medium heat and skim off any scum that appears.

Add the pearl barley, reduce the heat and cook gently, covered, for 1 hour.

Add the prepared vegetables and season well with salt and pepper.
Continue to cook for a further hour. Remove from the heat and allow
to cool slightly.

Remove the meat from the saucepan using a slotted spoon and strip
the meat from the bones. Discard the bones and any fat or gristle.
Place the meat back in the saucepan and leave to cool thoroughly,
then refrigerate overnight.

Scrape the solidified fat off the surface of the soup. Re-heat, season
with salt and pepper to taste and serve piping hot, garnished with the
parsley scattered over the top.

EASY
 SERVES 4
 **20 MINUTES +**
1 HOUR
MARINATING
 35 MINUTES

beef & bean soup

2 tbsp vegetable oil
1 large onion,
   finely chopped
2 garlic cloves,
   finely chopped
1 green pepper, deseeded
   and sliced
2 carrots, sliced

400 g/14 oz canned
   black-eyed beans
225 g/8 oz fresh
   beef mince
1 tsp each of ground
   cumin, chilli powder
   and paprika
¼ cabbage, sliced

225 g/8 oz tomatoes,
   peeled and chopped
600 ml/1 pint beef stock
salt and pepper

Heat the oil in a large saucepan over a medium heat. Add the onion
and garlic and cook, stirring frequently, for 5 minutes, or until softened.
Add the pepper and carrots and cook for a further 5 minutes.

Meanwhile, drain the beans, reserving the liquid from the can. Place
two-thirds of the beans, reserving the remainder, in a food processor
or blender with the bean liquid and process until smooth.

Add the mince to the saucepan and cook, stirring constantly, to break
up any lumps, until well browned. Add the spices and cook, stirring,
for 2 minutes. Add the cabbage, tomatoes, stock and puréed beans and
season to taste with salt and pepper. Bring to the boil, then reduce the
heat, cover and simmer for 15 minutes, or until the vegetables are tender.

Stir in the reserved beans, cover and simmer for a further 5 minutes.
Ladle the soup into warmed soup bowls and serve.

pork & vegetable broth

1 tbsp chilli oil
1 garlic clove, chopped
3 spring onions, trimmed
and sliced
1 red pepper, deseeded
and finely sliced
2 tbsp cornflour
1 litre/1¾ pints
vegetable stock
1 tbsp soy sauce

2 tbsp rice wine or dry
sherry
150 g/5½ oz pork
fillet, sliced
1 tbsp finely grated
lemongrass
1 small red chilli, deseeded
and finely chopped
1 tbsp grated fresh
root ginger

salt and pepper
115 g/4 oz fine egg
noodles
200 g/7 oz canned water
chestnuts, drained
and sliced
fresh green salad and
fresh crusty bread,
to serve

Heat the oil in a large saucepan. Add the garlic and spring onions and cook over a medium heat, stirring, for 3 minutes, until slightly softened. Add the red pepper and cook for a further 5 minutes, stirring. In a bowl, mix the cornflour with enough of the stock to make a smooth paste, then stir it into the pan. Cook, stirring, for 2 minutes. Stir in the remaining stock and the soy sauce and rice wine, then add the pork, lemongrass, chilli and ginger. Season with salt and pepper. Bring to the boil, then lower the heat and simmer for 25 minutes.

Bring a separate saucepan of water to the boil, add the noodles and cook for 3 minutes. Remove from the heat, drain, then add the noodles to the soup along with the water chestnuts. Cook for a further 2 minutes, then remove from the heat and ladle into serving bowls. Serve with a fresh green salad and crusty bread.

EASY **SERVES 4**  **30 MINUTES + 30 MINUTES COOLING** **1 HOUR 30 MINUTES**

middle eastern soup
with harissa

2 aubergines
3 tbsp olive oil
6 lamb shanks
1 small onion, chopped
400 ml/14 fl oz
  chicken stock
2 litres/3½ pints water
400 g/14 oz sweet
  potato, cut into chunks

5-cm/2-inch piece
  cinnamon stick
1 tsp ground cumin
2 tbsp chopped fresh
  coriander
HARISSA
2 red peppers, roasted,
  peeled, deseeded
  and chopped

½ tsp coriander seeds,
  dry-fried
25 g/1 oz fresh red
  chillies, chopped
2 garlic cloves, chopped
2 tsp caraway seeds
olive oil
salt

Preheat the oven to 200°C/400°F/Gas Mark 6. Prick the aubergines, place on a baking sheet and bake for 1 hour. When cool, peel and chop.

Heat the oil in a saucepan. Add the lamb and cook until browned. Add the onion, stock and water. Bring to the boil. Reduce the heat and simmer for 1 hour.

For the harissa, process the peppers, coriander seeds, chillies, garlic and caraway seeds in a food processor. With the motor running, add enough oil to make a paste. Season, then spoon into a jar. Cover with oil, seal and chill.

Remove the shanks from the stock, cut off the meat and chop. Add the sweet potato, cinnamon and cumin to the stock, bring to the boil, cover and simmer for 20 minutes. Discard the cinnamon and process the mixture in a food processor with the aubergine. Return to the saucepan, add the lamb and coriander and heat until hot. Serve with the harissa.

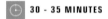

sweetcorn &
smoked chilli soup

1 tbsp corn oil
2 onions, chopped
550 g/1 lb 4 oz frozen
  sweetcorn kernels,
  thawed
600 ml/1 pint
  chicken stock
425 ml/15 fl oz milk

4 chipotle chillies,
  deseeded and
  finely chopped
2 garlic cloves,
  finely chopped
salt
55 g/2 oz thinly sliced
  chorizo sausage

2 tbsp lime juice
2 tbsp chopped
  fresh coriander

Heat the oil in a large, heavy-based saucepan. Add the onions and cook over a low heat, stirring occasionally, for 5 minutes, or until softened. Stir in the sweetcorn, cover and cook for a further 3 minutes.

Add the stock, half the milk, the chillies and garlic and season with salt. Bring to the boil, reduce the heat, then cover and simmer for 15–20 minutes.

Stir in the remaining milk. Reserve about 175 ml/6 fl oz of the soup solids, draining off as much liquid as possible. Transfer the remaining soup to a food processor or blender and process to a coarse purée.

Return the soup to the saucepan and stir in the reserved soup solids, the chorizo, lime juice and coriander. Re-heat to simmering point, stirring constantly. Ladle into warmed bowls and serve immediately.

pulses, grains & noodles

Comforting soups containing beans, grains and noodles are heartwarming at any time of the year. Many of the recipes in this section use canned beans because they are convenient, but you can use dried if you prefer. Simply adjust the soaking and cooking times accordingly. The times vary according to the type of bean, so always check the instructions on the packet. Whether you use canned or dried beans, these soups are highly nutritious, and many need only fresh crusty bread to transform them into satisfying meals in themselves.

spiced lentil & vegetable soup

1 tsp vegetable or olive oil
1 tsp mild curry paste
1 clove garlic, peeled and
  crushed or finely chopped
350ml/12fl oz vegetable
  stock
1 medium onion, chopped
30g/1¼ oz dried red lentils

1 medium carrot, peeled
  and chopped
1 small parsnip or potato,
  peeled and chopped
1 medium stalk celery,
  chopped
1 tsp tomato purée

Heat the oil in a lidded, non-stick saucepan, add the curry paste and garlic and stir over a low heat for 1 minute.

Add the stock and stir to combine, then add the rest of the ingredients and bring to a simmer over a medium-high heat.

Turn the heat down, put the lid on and cook for 40–50 minutes or until the lentils are tender.

Remove half or all the soup from the pan and purée in an electric blender. Return the soup to the pan and reheat gently to serve.

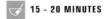
minestrone

2 tbsp olive oil
2 garlic cloves, chopped
2 red onions, chopped
75 g/2¾ oz Parma ham,
  sliced
1 red pepper, deseeded
  and chopped
1 orange pepper,
  deseeded and chopped

400 g/14 oz canned
  chopped tomatoes
1 litre/1¾ pints
  vegetable stock
1 celery stick, trimmed
  and sliced
400 g/14 oz canned
  borlotti beans
100 g/3½ oz green leafy
  cabbage, shredded

75 g/2¾ oz frozen peas,
  defrosted
1 tbsp chopped fresh parsley
salt and pepper
75 g/2¾ oz dried vermicelli
freshly grated Parmesan
  cheese, to garnish
fresh crusty bread,
  to serve

Heat the oil in a large saucepan. Add the garlic, onions and Parma ham and cook over a medium heat, stirring, for 3 minutes, until slightly softened. Add the red and orange peppers and the chopped tomatoes and cook for a further 2 minutes, stirring. Stir in the stock, then add the celery. Drain and add the borlotti beans along with the cabbage, peas and parsley. Season with salt and pepper. Bring to the boil, then lower the heat and simmer for 30 minutes.

Add the vermicelli to the pan. Cook for a further 10–12 minutes, or according to the instructions on the packet. Remove from the heat and ladle into serving bowls. Garnish with freshly grated Parmesan and serve with fresh crusty bread.

VERY EASY **SERVES 4**  **10 - 15 MINUTES + 10 MINUTES COOLING** **45 MINUTES**

pea & ham soup

1 tbsp butter	200 g/7 oz lean smoked	cooked ham, chopped and
1 onion, sliced	ham, chopped	sprigs of fresh tarragon,
1 leek, trimmed and sliced	1 bay leaf	to garnish
1 litre/1¾ pints	1 tbsp chopped	fresh crusty rolls,
vegetable stock	fresh tarragon	to serve
450 g/1 lb freshly shelled	salt and pepper	
peas, or frozen peas,	4 tbsp double cream	
defrosted		

Melt the butter in a large saucepan over a medium heat. Add the onion and cook, stirring, for 3 minutes, until slightly softened. Add the leek and cook for a further 2 minutes, stirring. Stir in the stock, then add the peas, ham, bay leaf and tarragon. Season with salt and pepper. Bring to the boil, then lower the heat and simmer for 30 minutes. Remove from the heat and discard the bay leaf. Leave to cool for 10 minutes.

Transfer half of the soup into a food processor and blend until smooth. Return to the pan with the rest of the soup, stir in the cream and cook over a low heat for a further 5 minutes.

Remove the soup from the heat and ladle into serving bowls. Garnish with chopped ham and sprigs of fresh tarragon and serve with fresh crusty rolls.

VERY EASY **SERVES 4**  **15 MINUTES +** **8 HOURS** **SOAKING** **2 HOURS** **45 MINUTES**

tunisian garlic &
chickpea soup

8 tbsp olive oil
12 garlic cloves, very
  finely chopped
350 g/12 oz chickpeas,
  soaked overnight in cold
  water and drained
2.5 litres/4½ pints water
1 tsp ground cumin

1 tsp ground coriander
2 carrots, very finely
  chopped
2 onions, very finely
  chopped
6 celery sticks, very
  finely chopped
juice of 1 lemon

salt and pepper
4 tbsp chopped
  fresh coriander

Heat half the oil in a large, heavy-based saucepan. Add the garlic and cook over a low heat, stirring frequently, for 2 minutes. Add the chickpeas to the saucepan with the measured water, cumin and ground coriander. Bring to the boil, then reduce the heat and simmer for 2½ hours, or until tender.

Meanwhile, heat the remaining oil in a separate saucepan. Add the carrots, onions and celery, cover and cook over a medium-low heat, stirring occasionally, for 20 minutes.

Stir the vegetable mixture into the saucepan of chickpeas. Transfer about half the soup to a food processor or blender and process until smooth. Return the purée to the saucepan, add about half the lemon juice and stir. Taste and add more lemon juice as required. Season to taste with salt and pepper. Ladle into warmed bowls, sprinkle with the fresh coriander and serve.

VERY EASY **SERVES 4**  **15 MINUTES + 10 MINUTES COOLING** **55 MINUTES**

mixed bean soup with gruyère

1 tbsp extra-virgin olive oil
3 garlic cloves, finely chopped
4 spring onions, trimmed and sliced
200 g/7 oz mushrooms, sliced
1 litre/1¾ pints vegetable stock

1 large carrot, peeled and chopped
400 g/14 oz canned mixed beans, drained
800 g/1 lb 12 oz canned chopped tomatoes
1 tbsp chopped fresh thyme
1 tbsp chopped fresh oregano

salt and pepper
175 g/6 oz Gruyère cheese, grated
4 tbsp double cream
swirls of single cream and finely chopped spring onions, to garnish
thick slices of fresh bread, to serve

Heat the oil in a large saucepan over a medium heat. Add the garlic and spring onions and cook, stirring, for 3 minutes, until slightly softened. Add the mushrooms and cook for a further 2 minutes, stirring. Stir in the stock, then add the carrot, mixed beans, chopped tomatoes and herbs. Season with salt and pepper. Bring to the boil, then lower the heat and simmer for 30 minutes. Remove from the heat and leave to cool for 10 minutes.

Transfer into a food processor and blend until smooth. Return to the pan and stir in the cheese. Cook for a further 10 minutes, then stir in the cream. Cook for 5 minutes, then remove from the heat and ladle into serving bowls. Garnish with swirls of cream and chopped or sliced spring onions. Serve with slices of fresh bread.

VERY EASY **SERVES 4** **20 MINUTES + 10 MINUTES COOLING** **50 MINUTES**

tomato, rice & tarragon soup

2 tbsp olive oil
2 garlic cloves, chopped
2 red onions, chopped
1 red pepper, deseeded
  and chopped
8 tomatoes, skinned,
  deseeded and chopped
1 litre/1¾ pints
  vegetable stock
1 celery stick, trimmed
  and sliced

175 g/6 oz brown rice
1 tbsp chopped
  fresh tarragon
salt and pepper
100 ml/3½ fl oz
  double cream
sprigs of fresh tarragon,
  to garnish
fresh crusty bread,
  to serve

Heat the oil in a large saucepan. Add the garlic and onions and cook over a medium heat, stirring, for 3 minutes, until slightly softened. Add the red pepper and the tomatoes and cook for a further 2 minutes, stirring. Stir in the stock, then add the celery, rice and tarragon. Season with salt and pepper. Bring to the boil, then lower the heat and simmer for 30 minutes. Remove from the heat and leave to cool for 10 minutes.

Transfer half of the soup into a food processor and blend until smooth. Return to the pan with the rest of the soup and cook for 5 minutes. Stir in the cream and cook for a further 5 minutes. Remove from the heat and ladle into serving bowls. Garnish with sprigs of fresh tarragon and serve with fresh crusty bread.

VERY EASY   **SERVES 4**   **15 MINUTES**   **5 MINUTES**

tofu & noodle broth

1 tbsp sesame oil
1 garlic clove, chopped
4 spring onions, trimmed
  and sliced
1 small red chilli,
  deseeded and
  finely chopped
50 g/1¾ oz shiitake
  mushrooms, sliced

50 g/1¾ oz chestnut
  mushrooms, sliced
1 tbsp rice wine
2 tsp soy sauce
2 tbsp chopped
  fresh coriander
1 litre/1¾ pints
  vegetable stock
75 g/2¾oz dried fine

egg noodles
100 g/3½ oz firm tofu,
  drained and cut into
  small cubes
salt and pepper
chopped fresh coriander,
  to garnish

Heat the oil in a large wok or saucepan over a high heat. Add the
garlic, spring onions and chilli and stir-fry for 1 minute, until slightly
softened. Add the mushrooms, rice wine, soy sauce, coriander and
stock and bring to the boil. Lower the heat, add the noodles and
simmer for 3 minutes.

Add the tofu and season with salt and pepper. Remove from the heat,
then transfer into individual serving bowls. Garnish with chopped fresh
coriander and serve with fresh crusty bread.

index